And Then Came The Flood

A collection of sorts by Lacey Roop

Roop, Lacey
1st edition.
ISBN: 978-0-615-68440-6

Edited by Jacob Dodson, Casey B. Renz, and Kevin W. Burke
Interior layout design by Amy McDonnold
Cover design by Amy McDonnold and Lacey Roop

Printed in Texas, USA

Timber Mouse Publishing
Austin, TX
www.timbermouse.com

To contact the author, please email laceyroop@hotmail.com

"I am sure people tell you this constantly, but if you looked up 'incredibly beautiful' in the dictionary, there would be a picture of you."
—*Jonathan Safran Foer*

SUMMER

Let's forget all of the days and rules and what we were supposed to do with ourselves and just be who we are.

SHARK BOY

Make me into a mountain!
Said the boy.

Make me into a dove with iron wings
so if someone shoots me I won't feel it,
I'll just keep flying.

Make me into something God hears.
I want to speak every language
because I know he has to understand at least one.

Give me arms stronger than my father's
so I can stand-up to him next time.
Give me a mind that won't forget things worth remembering.
Give me the things you know you'll never use
because all things have purpose;
I just want answers,
He says.

This boy is the accumulation of every spirit who refused to quit burning.
He carries the sun in his shadow.
He just turned 7.

He tells me that he is supposed to close his eyes
when he sees something bad,
but he tried it once, and only had his eyes open twice that day.

He only had his eyes open long enough
to see the oak tree by his home
wave goodbye to him as he walked himself to school alone,
and noticed a blue bird sharing a worm
with a black bird which made him wonder
why color matters to people?
I want to be the wind.
He says.

I want to be the feeling that gives others goosebumps.
I want my fingerprint to be in the shape of a dragonfly.
I want to be cobalt blue.

His eyes are as innocent as the inside of angels.
He wants to be everything he can imagine.
Out of all the things I can think of I want to be more like him.
He looks up to me as if the entire universe is my lover
just because I can read the *Encyclopedia Britannica*

and pronounce the names of dinosaurs.
He thinks I am a hero and it makes me sad.
I know we all had thoughts like his when we were younger
but it seems like with every candle we blow out on our birthdays
something greater than flames disappears.

You know everything!
He says.

No, no,
I say.

I only know what I have been taught.
You know what you feel—
that's far more important.

His head is still arched up
looking at me, smiling,
even though he doesn't really understand
what it is I am trying to tell him.
That's not the part that scares me:
It is knowing that someday he will.

It is knowing that in the next ten years he will be taught
that no human can be made into a mountain.
That the sun and moon don't really chase him around
they just appear that way.
It is knowing that his heart will be broken
by someone who didn't love him
as much as he loved them.

That his perception of the world might change
from thinking of it
as a ginormous place to play
with too many trees he won't get to climb,
too many puddles of water he won't get to jump in
because he ran out of time,
to calculating how much money he can make
and avoiding water holes so he won't get his dress shoes dirty.

I stare at him.

I stare at his entire body from the white roots of his hair follicles
to the bottoms of his LA Gears that light-up when he walks
trying to understand him.

He stares at me doing the same.
He isn't wondering what I'm going to be.
He is trying to understand who I am,
now.

I want to tell him to not grow-up.
To quit blowing out the candles on his birthdays
but I know that will only set him up for disappointment because

age is inevitable;
our perception is what changes.

So instead I ask him,
Do you like to swim, kid?

And with a tongue of a sage the seven-year-old boy tells me this,
Yeah! It's my favorite thing. We can play sharks and mermaids.
I can be the shark and you can be the mermaid!

As he grabs my hand and leads me to the water.

It is within that moment I come to understand
myself and this life, and I watch the boy grow up
to be something other than what he is.

He is a shark.
Who lives in the mountains.
And I a mermaid—

too bad reality can't accept us for who we truly are.

AMERICAN DOLL

August 1962.
In an interview with Marilyn Monroe
Ms. Magazine gleefully asked her,
How does it feel to be a sex symbol?

Her response,
A sex symbol becomes a thing...
I just hate to be a thing.

Oh Marilyn.
I know you never asked for your bones.
What a shame we made you pay
for how your skin stretched over them.
Symmetry we called it. Perfect, even.
You stitchless beauty—
our own American doll.

We hung you in the headlights of Hollywood,
printed you on 8x10s,
made you as common as a cough.

At the advent of the color motion picture
you shifted the beauty paradigm,
caused brunettes to rip fistfuls of hair out hoping
it would bloom back blonde.
People migrated towards you as if you were the gold rush.

We did not care for Norma Jean,
so we made Marilyn Monroe.
You became our epidemic.

It was all your fault, sweetheart,
Some said.

The way we scanned your body like an item to be put in a bag.
Told you that what you had to say was as interesting as a dial tone.

You were too pretty to be considered the shy girl,
mistook your quietness for either stuck-up or dumb.

You don't need a brain, baby, with a body like that,
Is what they told you.

It has been 50 years since your death
and you have become what you never wanted to be.

An emblem.
An icon.
A pin-up pimped for all things sexy.

Your skeleton a mound of silt, knuckles gravel in a tomb
yet your epithet still howls

Blond bombshell
Honey
Sweetie
Baby

A person turned placard.

You never wanted your bones.
Yet you are still strewn across billboards.
An imprint on a Visa Platinum™.
We used you like a napkin to wipe ourselves clean with;
your skin was *that* distracting.

We never thought to ask how you felt in it.
Instead we proudly opened the curtain
and announced you *sex symbol*
while the men of your era were declared heartthrobs
despite all the Joe DiMaggio punches
you received from a husband who
we deemed hero.

The only help you received from producers
was this piece of advice,
Duck if he tries to hit you in the face, doll—
that's just too pretty to bang up.

We made you as secondhand as a receipt.
A proof of purchase
that you are just some thing,
girl.

It is no wonder you had trouble sleeping.
Afraid that if you closed your eyes for too long
women would come in and slit your silhouette
and attempt to stitch themselves in it.

Men would ecstatically rape your shadow. You,
Marilyn, were that sexy.

We couldn't help it.

As soon as you curved we felt that
your body was ours for the taking,
squeezed you like an avocado to see if you were ripe enough,
peeled you like a fruit;
we thought you honeydew, apricot.

You were supple, sensuous,
the thought of being tangled with you muddled men,
caused women to curse their bones
for the way they curved under their own skin.

Stop crying! Why are you such an ungrateful bitch?
Don't you know that people would kill to be you,
Marilyn.

Because who would have ever thought
that you would kill yourself
to not?

WATERMELON SEASON

Lord, help the poor and needy in this land, in this land.
Lord, help the slaving man, in this land, in this land.
Lord, help when that rain gonna come, when the rain gonna fall down.
Lord, help when that rain gonna come, when the rain gonna fall
and swallow this town.

The storm swallowed the town the year the watermelon bloomed.

The rain came like a freight-train,
blew the wind in like a bad omen,
turned cattle skulls into confetti.
The people watched the ground flip upside down—
everything f-l-y-iiiiii-n-ggggg.

Tupelo, MS. April 5th, 1936.
The date for the 4th worst tornado in US history.
My mawmaw hid her babies
under the floorboards of a sharecropper shack,
said no one saw it coming.
Thought it was the devil himself
the way the sky coughed open;
turned jet-black.

Elvis himself was found under the debris
barely one year old
coughing and crying already
filled with all the Blues that storm blew in him.

217 dead, 700 wounded
by the 3 block funnel
that plowed through the town.

That storm cloud just sucked up and spit out
bodies as if they were sunflower seeds.

The black part of town known as Shake Rag
completely disappeared.
A bank sits there now,
on top of all the colored families that got shoveled
under a signpost that now reads 399 E Commerce St.
Appropriate they give the street that divided skin
a name associated with trade and dollar bills.

The only thing left of Shake Rag now
are cigar boxes and guitar strings,

but I swear when I go back there
I can still hear their hymn in the howl of the wind.

My mawmaw was 27 when that funnel fell like a fist,
Punching through everything they built.

It was the year of watermelon, she said.
I couldn't tell if the chunks I saw whirling in the wind
was the fruit that was growing or the inside of men.

It took years before things were rebuilt and put back
but my mawmaw's spine still shakes when those sirens sound,
and she hasn't touched a watermelon ever since.

They aren't as sweet as they once were
with all that salt in the skin of 'em.

Sometimes when I go back home
I hear her coughing up an old gospel song.
My grandma says it's because of all the cigarette smoke
but I think that it's because she's still
got that rainwater in her throat.

She's very old now.

I close my eyes when she sings.

There is a story in her sound.

If I listen real close it goes something like

Lord, help the poor and needy in this land, in this land, in this land.
Lord, help the slaving man, in this land, in this land.
Lord, help when the rain gonna come, in this land, in this land.
Lord, help when the rain gonna fall, when the rain gonna fall
and swallow us all in this town,
in this town.

A FIELD TRIP BACK TO THE 3RD GRADE

At five years old I changed my name to Rocky
because I thought it was much more masculine than Lacey.

I traded all my barbie dolls in for GI-Joe's & basketballs.
When my mom tried to dress me in dresses
I told her that the best thing about 'em was that
it made it easier for me to pee
while standing up.

For the entirety of third grade I wasn't
allowed to participate in recess
because of a parent-teacher conference
my mom and Mrs. Baker had
over how to get Lacey to realize that she is, in fact,
a girl.

Mrs. Baker told me that if I were going to continue to play basketball
with the boys I was gonna have to let them win or not play at all
because it was just too confusing for everyone
how such a
Pretty.
Little.
Girl.
could be so,
strong?

I sat on the sidewalk all by myself that year
and watched my classmates play,
I guess this is why I've been so comfortable with loneliness;
this is what happens when you spend most of your life
holding your own hand.

18 years have passed since I was a 3rd grader
but just the the other day I was invited to read
at an elementary school
a story I wrote about a little lion cub
who got in trouble and was made fun of
because of who he loved.

At the end of class I was curious about
what love meant to them so I asked

and 6 year old Nikka told me this,
If you wanna learn to love better,
you should start with a friend you hate.

Noelle said, *Love is when you tell someone*
you like their shirt and they wear it everyday.

Bobby added, *Love is what's in the room with you at Christmas*
if you stop opening presents and listen.

I think if we wanna make the world a more understanding place
we should stop indoctrinating hate
and begin to listen to the wisdom coming from the ones
who still chew with their baby teeth.

For not one of the kids in the class that day
said love had anything to do with gender,
but everything to do with the feeling
you get when a person you like
walks into a room.

Ask Danny - age 9 - who said love is as simple as a garden going bloom.

It's the firework boom inside of you!

It's why I had to move 2,200 miles away from my birthplace
before I ever felt home.

Yet there are still days I can't forget
every time that my Bible-belt town threw the buckle at my back
trying to beat the boy in me out;
wanting to know if I bled pink or blue.

In high school, I cut myself once to see
if I could get the feelings I had out
as if attraction is something you can help.

It was hard living in a town where being different
scarlet letters you wrong,
but what I know now is that you've gotta sing your unique,
wear your awkward strong,
and never be ashamed of the love you may contain for someone.

I was reminded of this while reading to that room full of kids
who just sat there and listened with no care

as to who or what I should be.
They just hugged me and asked if I thought
that the little lion will ever stop
getting in trouble and made fun of for who he loves.

I said, *I don't know.*

I hope so.

I've got my fingers crossed
that the grown-ups will see love like ya'll see it one day.

BECOMING THE PANACEA

The scientist calls you a *cataclysmic alchemist,*
but I hear you have healing hands,
and I think we all need a softer spot to land.

Tell me what's the point in your math and elixirs?

Why are we so preoccupied
in figuring out the science in stars
instead of appreciating them
for not making the night feel so lonely?

Let me get lost in the distance.

While everyone is fighting over becoming
that diamond in the rough
I'd just like to be a pebble because there is no ugly,
only variations of beautiful.

It is in the chipped, the burned, the broken.
The disfigured, dismembered, disenchanted.

Don't chastise the dreamers for believing in things
you deem untrue and make-believe.

Despite what scientists say,
I know there are trumpets in our tendons.

In a world that is trying to make sense of it all
let us not forget the importance
of those who understand the art of pretending
before the imagination police come to take that away.

If I tell you I've got wings in my scapulaslings
do not condemn me for things you can't see
because the pendulum swings both ways,

I can't see your God.
But I don't condemn you for believing
in something different than me.

Let me have my waterfalls,
open arms,
star-crawls, and orangedust sunups.

'Cuz lately the earth seems so far away
with all this concrete and gridlock,
convenience and enterprise,
even the birds are having a hard time
flying through their own sky
because of all the shit we have in it.

A scientist can tell you everything about *How*
but cannot answer *Why?*

We have been taught that your alchemy is archaic alchemist,
but I have heard you've discovered methods of transmuting
baser metals to gold.

That you can make the mundane magnificent
with your panacea palms.
If this is the case will you and the scientist
quit referencing only past/future
and work together this time
to fix what is present
before we outrun the earth with our invention
until there are no more soft spots for us to call

home.

WHAT'S SO CRAZY ABOUT HAVING WAVES IN YOUR VEINS?

...and they tell me that I can't keep the ocean in my ribs,
but I do.

That dangerous things live there.
That there have been stories of
barracuda monsters,
octopuses with 15 tentacle, testicle thingies,
whales that will swallow you,
and sharks that can't wait to taste a human.

But despite all of this the manatees and mermaids
are enough to keep the waves in my veins,
so I'm swimming.

I got the touch of beautiful women in my shivers;
even though I don't know the meaning of love
I know the feeling of fingers
and that's enough to get me by

for now.

In the wind there are words I have a hard time catching,
but I'm trying my best to grab 'em
and keep 'em in my pocket
so when I get home I'll have more poems
to write and stories to tell because

every day is a new chance to look at the same things differently.

To stand with no umbrella in the rain
because the rain is just the sky
wanting to touch you.

Listen to the birds and crickets chirping away
because everything with sound has a song to sing
and anything that breathes has something to say

So listen.

Just because this *thing* called *reality* tells you
that you can't breathe stars,

snuggle with clouds,
french kiss raindrops,
or grow flowers in your hands.

You can!

People told me that I couldn't do a lot of things;
I believed them for a while but I'm doing them now.

I'm practicing hugs and handshakes
because that's what saves people.
I never believed that refraining from
cursing or saying your prayers
would get you any closer to heaven
or any further from hell.

Don't be afraid to pull the bricks from your feet
and skip to your next location,
because the greatest distance, I swear, is still the one within you.

Give the finger to self-reservation
and begin to be the thing that you always wanted to be
but was too afraid to do.

Keep sonnets in your sinews,
rest in your lover's whispers,
snuggle with change until it becomes your constant,
learn to look at yourself in the mirror at any time of the day
and smile; finding that the definition of beauty
is in your own reflection.

Because in the end who is to say what is true?

Who is to tell you who you should love?
Who is to tell you who you should be?
Who is to tell you what is real and what to believe?

Reality was only created to make another category
that would define a certain group of people as crazy.

I know what I feel and
I'm beginning to understand who I am.

I'm just a girl

who keeps the ocean in my ribs and the waves in my veins
despite all of the terrible things that people say it contains.

But I think at the end of the day
we are all just swimming.

PIANOLAND

Once there was a city of pianos.

It was a pianoland and we were the notes and we were the fingers and we were the fingers that hit the tusks of keys that made the sound of roaring rivers. We played the tide until the moon came. It shook us like shivers.

We were small and big and beautiful and senseless and above all—

Alive.

In the piano orchard we blew like sheets hung on clothespins during a southern July. The sweat came out from the folds of our skin; how perfect we glistened. I watched the way the noise rose from the pianos you punched like smoke and snow and steam.

It was an acrobatic act of keys— the sound of song— and all I wanted was to wrap myself up in it like a tourniquet or swallow the moment whole, keep it like an anchor in my belly, some permanent instant you wouldn't dare to let go.

On the stool you swayed like a drift,
that discerning swagger,
and I swear I'd stay forever
if such a thing existed.

In the piano orchard you can put your dreams on a sheet and play until the sun sets on your shoulders and your shadow stands erected while the moon comes like a whisper setting you aflame in its afterglow.

And time doesn't ever come or stay or happen,
it just is,
like the way it's supposed to be.
A fluidity of moments.
A changing constant, or a constant changing.

I don't know anymore since I've been stuck on one end of the city banging out notes like a burning kettledrum, and I don't care that I don't know what I'm doing.

I've never been a piano player.

I don't know all the notes or keys or sounds or riffs
that you and I do with each other.
The notes you bang, baby, are the color of thunder,

and I'm wonderin' how it is that this piano town is spinning like a world
we once knew but never felt we belonged to.
And every key you hit sounds like you're either trying to let go or hold on.

You pound each key like you are asking a question
and I don't know what you are asking,
but even if I did I don't think I'd have the answer for you.

Maybe, just maybe,
there is some glimmer of glory
in the uncertainty of not knowing it all.

I've slept too many nights hoping to lasso dreams
so I could throw them into the face of the sun.

Come morning,

I will build a city. A pianoland. An orchard of pianos. Where we can be
small and big and beautiful and senseless. You play your roaring river,
wildeyed, and alive.
I'll sit in the distance. Somewhere buried in the silence
swallowed by what I always imagined we could become,
while you kept believing in all that
we couldn't be.

FREMONT, WA

She tells me that one day she will live in Fremont, Washington
because that is the center of the universe.

But I wanna tell her that you don't always
have to be in the center of everything,
I'm sure people standing in the middle of the world still
miss things.

The problem with me is that I think too much
and never say enough.

I get stuck in my stutter-steps,
choke on words the size of sunsets that get garbled in my mouth.

I can't speak declarative sentences to her.

So instead I communicate through metaphors
careful not to do anything too sudden that would make her feel
uncomfortable around me.

Refrain from letting my body drape her body
like chapel paintings trying to understand God,
because those are the only two things
I could dedicate my entire life to and never understand completely.

Gemini—

I think your heads are pretty.
It's just hard to understand the things you tell me
with those two tongues you have.

If I had the courage I'd ask her if she remembers
painting pictures on my belly in her favorite color green.
Trading poems for stories while lying in my bed,
placing names on the stars that dangled overhead.

I slept in her shivers trying to get us to fit;
she grabbed my hand, placed it on my chest, and said,

*You should stop thinking so much and start to feel
the parts that are dancing instead.*

But what happens to hearts after they break?
Do they repair themselves or evaporate?

I built walls stronger than Babylon.
but even the most invincible metals
are still no match for a wrecking ball.

She placed hooks in me,
ripping out parts that I never knew I had.

And sometimes I wonder if it gets heavy for her?

Holding all those hearts in such small hands.
If it makes her feel like she matters because so many people care.

If I could pull the crosses she bears
and carve them into my bones
I would.

Wear her shame prouder than expensive armor
reassuring her that her flaws leave me breathless;
they make perfection jealous.

I would take the bad men who chase her in her nightmares
and gladly place them in my head.

She can give me all of her ghosts and goblins.

I'll cut Juliets out of my skin for her
to show her that not every Romeo has to be a man.

That we all come in different forms,
but that I do understand
that I may not be the *thing*
she is into.

But I can't help but taste Venus in her lips when we kiss,
catching dragonflies in my ribs,
wanting to show her that this is what she did...

I'd etch a treasure map in my thumbs,
carve lips in my wrists,
in hopes that if we ever shook hands again
she would find the best parts about me she missed.

I want to tell her that I'm not like everyone,
But neither is anyone else
I guess.

When she moves on to Washington I will be happy for her.
I'll try my best to understand.

But a part of me will wish
that even when she is living in the center of the universe,

in the middle of everything,

the one thing she will miss
will be me.

AUTUMN

built my skeleton out of guardrails
welded padlocks in my bones
I'm constructing an art called distance
it is a delicate issue—

the space between our palms.

OPPOSITE DIRECTIONS

Remember the time I told you I liked you and you didn't say anything?
You just smiled.

It took another 17 days before you told me that you liked me back,
and on the nights in between that, I sat in the middle of my kitchen floor
with a 6 pack just wonderin' what it was you were so hesitant about?

What part of liking me scared you?

Over coffee & cigarettes we make talk not because we are interested in
what we have to say but because it is an innocent excuse to see each
other. I ask your opinion about organic apples, *Waking Life,* and the
zombie apocalypse because it's Austin and these are the sorts of things
people talk about...

You look at me so cute and confused like while we rendezvous up and
down the city streets discussing how fucked up the world is 'cuz that
is what people in their twenty-somethings do with our Good Morning
America, angst in the afternoon outlook, middle-finger extended the way
we hold questions like balloons and drift...

We've got fists in our eyes and that's such a bleak way to see things so I
brush my hand against yours while we are walking through the city and
pretend I didn't mean to touch you, but really, we both know I did.

You look at me slightly confused but awfully cute and ask,
Where to next? What are we doing? Where do you wanna go?
And I hate when these questions arise because indecisiveness is my
downfall, so I say with a mouth full of cotton,
tongue heavy as a bag full of bricks,
*I don't know? I don't care. Whatever you want. We can go
     anywhere!*

But what I really wanted to say was nothing.

Just grab you by the waist
all James Dean and Clark Gable
and kiss you right there
in the middle of Congress Ave amidst the
buzzing traffic, lunch breakers, and dedicated joggers.

But to do this takes courage.

So instead we end up walkin' back to where we started.

A table and two chairs.

We stare at each other's lips trying to decide if we are going to kiss goodbye this time.

Our arms extend.

We hug.

So much distance between two pressed bodies is hard to understand. It is a long embrace.

We feel the muscles in our backs collapse.

My eyes are closed.
I don't know about yours.

I kiss your temple.

It is holy there.

I say *See you later.*
You say *Goodbye.*

We ride off in opposite directions
with each other's scent
still stuck to our clothes.

AN OPEN LETTER TO THOSE WHO KISS GIRLS

When a girl says, *kiss me,* be careful.
She may not know what she is asking.
She may not know what she wants.
Some girls never do.

Ask her what she wants.
Assure her there are no wrong answers.

If she says she needs time, give her all your clocks.
If it's space she wants, construct her a rocket;
send her there.

Mean what you say.
Girls do not like to be lied to.
Mean what you say.

Kiss her but do not expect anything.
Above all else, girls disdain expectations.

Do not discard her as *just another one*
or mistake her as a wonder carved from the skin of the moon.

Girls are special; not unique.

They are hair, hide.
Teeth, thumb.
Bone, brain.

Wondrous vessels composed of hellos, heartbeats.
Goodbyes, gums.

Their bodies shaped like cellos or pears.
As unpredictable and powerful as wind or waves.
Understand what I mean when I say,
welcome her crash with caution.

Tell her you appreciate her entirety, even the rust.
Build her a castle with the dust she's swept under the rug.
Undress her ghosts. Tell her, her ghouls are gorgeous.
Palm her phantoms. Do not treat her like a problem to solve.

You are not that advanced.

She is not a book to be read then placed back on the shelf.
A magazine to thumb through,
a letter to be opened or sent out.
Some 44cent stamp.

She is not an equation; do not treat her like a number.

Pull her close.
Follow her breath.
Study it.
Listen.

Kiss her like rain. Kiss her like spark. Kiss her like whisper.
Go slow. Let her hips guide you. Feel her meaningful. Thrust gentle.

Move like you are giving something back
instead of taking something from her.

Never make her feel like she is an accident;
even if you hate her,
do not hate her.

Accept her misunderstood.

Understand her uncomfortable. Love her awkward. Adore her whole.
Respect her being. Embrace her difficult. Cuddle her complexity. Caress
her chaos. Hold her honest.

Take her broken; lick it perfect.

Let her know she has always been a jawdropper.

But do not put her on a pedestal;
you may like her too much to hurt herself if she falls.

When a girl says, *kiss me,*
be careful.

She may not know what she is asking.
And you may not anticipate the haunting
she could become
when she doesn't want you
anymore.

GENDER IS A UNIVERSE

While squatting down to take a piss I read,
gender is a universe and we are all stars.
Scribbled on the wall of a bathroom stall.

I was so in awe by this that I went home and poured myself a flask and
crawled on top the roof to ponder what I had read.
I stared with amazement at the vastness of constellations just wonderin'
if God has become an angry drunk because of the ignorance and intol-
erance he sees in us?

How we like to stereotype, nitpick, criticize, compare black and white,
judge each other based on our hairstyles and pant size.

I guess that's why every time I go out at night I always get asked,
Hey! Are you a dude or a dyke?

And all I wanna say is,
*Oh hi, dude bra'! Ummm, I don't know, how 'bout you ask your girlfriend
since she was the one who went down on me last night.*

But I refrain and say,
Well, I'm a little bit of both and sometimes neither.

Give him a hug then walk away while he stands there intrigued
still trying to figure me out,
and I'm not really offended as much as I am saddened
by how it never occurred to this guy
that people's sexual preference doesn't diminish the fact that we are still
human.

It's an atrocity that we still have to be reminded of this.
Did you know that it took nearly 300 years after
the first American settlement before
the white man recognized that black people have souls too?

I wonder if it is going to take 300 more before people
quit telling me that they think it's cute that I kiss girls.

As if my lifestyle is some trendy fashion statement,
gay 'till graduation bullshit,
like I'm a curious exhibitionist.

I wish my mom would quit telling me
this is a stage I'm going through

and recognize that this is a skin
her daughter has finally felt comfortable enough in
for me to tell her about girlfriends.

'Cuz from 2nd grade 'till I was a sophomore in college
I was taught to camouflage my feelings because the state of Mississippi
has it written that love can only exist between a man and a woman.
As if a state has the right to dictate who you want to spend the rest of
your life with.

But on nights when I'm sleeping next to someone soft
I can't help but wonder about the ones still struggling in my hometown
like Mikey,
who had to put a silencer over his heartbeat
because it thumped too loud whenever Andrew was in the room;
he was afraid that his church would condemn him.

Or Irene,
who used to dye her hair bright blue to distract
people from staring in dismay at her and Shay's interlocked fingers;
as if homosexuality was a disease instead of just another form of loving.

I think I might just crawl on top my roof and get drunk with God again
so he can hear me when I ask him to keep an eye out on
Irene and Mikey
or anyone else who is being taught
to be ashamed of themselves for their feelings.

Tonight I don't wanna have to explain myself.

I'm tired of having to explain myself.

I don't wanna be distinguished as gay, straight, lesbian,
queer, dude, or dyke

just *human.*

Because gender really is a universe
and we need to accept that we are all mere stars
a part of the same great galaxy.

THE PLACES YOU ARE AREN'T ALWAYS THE PLACES YOU'LL BE

I.
We broke glass with our knuckles to see who would cut the deepest.
Your wounds smelled like autumn or coins or ash;
Mine like pine or corduroy or mud.
Burned like whiskey in the back of a mouth,
Flowed like a thick sap,
the blood.

II.
When the scars healed we'd name 'em after the state we got 'em in.
Wrong turns come in the shape of Arkansas, Tennessee.
Split lips welcome! West Virginia, Missouri.
I got 'em for saying all the wrong things too perfectly;
some like to say I'm a bit of a smart-ass.

Fuck 'em.

Connecticut, I didn't jump fast enough.
New Mexico, I still got your railroad tracks in my fists.
That broken heart contour happened somewhere in Texas.
The canine tooth I carry in my back pocket is a reminder
That you don't kiss on the mouth,
and when I tried it, after a few pints too many,
you threw a jab so hard through my jawbone,
I woke up blacked out and lonely. I call that state
Mississippi.

III.
I quit drinking... tea.

IV.
If I didn't think about you as often as I do
I would have forgotten you by now.

V.
I know the answer to forgetting;
you have to admit what it is you don't want to remember first.
Once, in an effort to do this, I took a 34 hour shower.
Burned the bed sheets.
Decapitated the flowers.
Mistook hot water in a bowl for soup.
I didn't want to say I was starving.

Slept naked on the roof.
Wish I could say it was my roof. It wasn't.
Swallowed lightning bugs so you wouldn't pass me up again.
This is why I glow and talk the way that I do.

VI.
There's an Italian word that encapsulates the feeling of not wanting to forget even though you know how to. It's called malinconia. An interior satisfaction in some incompleteness that one unconsciously never wants to completely resolve.

VII.
I slit my tongue with a paring knife so I could pull your name from it. Throw it in the swamp. Leave it in the muck, in-behind the debris. I thought it was a good idea at the time until I had a mouth full of blood and heard that that you had changed your name. Again.

VII.
This body is my home.

If I open the door for you, would you take off your shoes and be careful where you step next time.

VIII.
Do you believe in next time?
Or would you agree with me when I say that to believe in them is to partake in the grandest lie. Time does not stand still. We do.
People have a tendency of passing each other bye.

IX.
I say this because I hear you live in a city below the sea. When the wind comes off the tide I sometimes smell autumn or coins or ash. This is how I know some don't heal, when I trace the outline of states in the form of scars wondering about the glass we broke, and if you ever miss the smell of pine.

X.
The lightning bugs won't come out of me.
Their home was my welcome. I glow from time to time.
I drink tea now.
Stopped with the whiskey.
There is a burn when I bleed.
I still carry that canine tooth, but I don't cry near as much
when I think about
Mississippi.

UP UP AND AWAY
(A SHORT, SHORT STORY)

I decided I was going to fly. I had dreamed enough about soaring above the ground, feet kicking clouds, and the taste of sky at high altitudes. I wasn't concerned anymore with wondering what the world must look like floating freely way up in the air. I wanted to feel it myself. Someone asked if I was going to buy an airplane ticket and go to Spain or Bali or wherever.

No. I said.
Another asked if skydiving or hang-gliding was what I had in mind.
No. I repeated.

There wasn't enough imagination in those methods of flying. Those were simply inventions that aided men and women with getting off the ground. I wanted to fly. On my own, alone, with no aiding apparatuses.

I spent months studying birds. I figured since they've been flying forever they surely knew the best way to do it. I read voraciously everything about sparrows and condors and hummingbirds and parrots and pigeons and so on. While walking in the park I came across a bluejay and asked him if he had any advice. The little guy chirped something like, *Do not fear falling,* or maybe it was *Do not fear failing.*

Easy thing for you to say, I thought. It is only human to fear both.

For a year I was deemed crazy bird-lady. You'd think that I must have kept a zoo full of birds with a nickname like that, but I did not. In fact, I oppose birds for pets. To keep something with wings in a cage seems cruel to me. I collected the feathers. It started small. One lump of mallard feathers stored in a mason jar. Then a pile of pigeon feathers suddenly covered my desk. I had cut holes in all my feather pillows and sprinkled them throughout my house. By the time I was finished there was no hardwood floor anymore.

After two years the feathers had devoured my home. Friends stopped coming over, my mother called incessantly certain I was going to jump off the roof and die. Even my neighbors made wagers on when they believed my house would just float away.

What is she planning to do with a house full of feathers?
Some people in the town asked.
She's crazy. She believes she is going to fly.

After three years I figured I had collected enough feathers. Every crevice of my house was infested with them. I'd open a can of beans and grackle feathers would spill out. The milk had somehow been replaced with dove feathers, and when I broke ice out of the ice-tray it didn't make a cracking sound, but a tweet.

Perhaps I had gone crazy?
Perhaps my house would break free from its foundation and fly away after all?

I had no more friends. My neighbors switched from being amused to terrified as soon as feathers began billowing out of my chimney. And my poor mother had completely stopped calling certain that I died a long time ago. I swam through the middle of my house (by this point I had to, it became impossible to walk) alone amongst a horde of bird feathers and wondered if living a dream was worth giving up a life?

Of course. I told myself. And you didn't give up your life, you are living your dream. This is why everyone is scared of you; they don't know how you did it.

It occurred to me then why so many people long to dream but are afraid to do so. If you fall for your dream, fall for anything really, you put yourself at risk to fail. This is terrifying to many. It was to me as well. I had spent 34 years of my life making ends meet while neglecting the very thing I wanted to do. Every morning I'd wake up eager for nighttime so I could go back to sleep and dream again. Every night it was the same dream, me soaring above in a sea of sky. I was tired of alarm clocks, gas stations, appointments, luncheons, checkbooks, junk mail...

After 3.5 years I opened my door. I didn't realize it was autumn and how much things had changed. The sky was a whole new color. The air was crisp with spice and smoke. I wondered if life had actually always been this color. If the past 34 autumns had smelled like this as well but since I had been so busy with meetings and phone calls and microwaves and traffic that I forgot to notice the hum of changing leaves.

As I stepped out on the porch I watched every house around me slowly raise their blinds. Their eyes big as chestnuts, mouths gapping holes all staring at me while forgetting the life around them. There I stood, the crazy bird-lady, in a coat of feathers. The sun felt like warm wool on my cheeks as I lifted my arms and slowly took off. When I looked back I saw the tiny hands of the town trying to catch the clouds of feathers swarming behind me. They looked like dreamchasers all running for something just barely out of reach.

We whittled wishes with the bones of fallen stars.
They called us dreamers;
wandering wonderers wondering
about the spin of the world
and the glow in our skin...

THE SPINNING WORLD

Some have this habit of looking out of windows and calling it *impossible.*

They look forward to sleeping so they can escape these feelings,
hug pillows tight, and dream of
letting go...

If I could paint a picture of all I could never hold in my hands
I'd name it *possible* and jump from this earth.
I'd somersault with the wind.
Put the dirt in my pockets and sail to the Arctic to show the Eskimos
that you can build castles out of anything.

People need hope.

Every non-believer believes in something
so doctor explain to me sunset because I know you felt it as a boy.
Mathematician, does your heart unwind at the spine
of certain books like problems you can't solve?

We consist of science and things that can't be explained by it.

The world is not a foreign place;
we are foreign to it.

It spins and spins and spins at 1,038mph on its orbit and
another 67,000mph more around the sun!

The average American will spend nearly 15 years of their life stagnant.
Waiting in line at grocery stores or traffic jams or on
phone calls with people who will never love you
as much as you have fallen in love with the idea that they might.

We wait.

Wishing for our chance to jump because so many of us
have responsibility tied to our ankles.
We clipped our wings years ago,
buried the pages of fables,
put away our crayons the moment
we got our driver's license.

Blocked out our imaginations with our BIG words
and plans for the future,
but the future is just an excuse
for you not to do incredible things with your life right now.

The minutes are ticking.
Moments build up on themselves.
Windows are here for you to know that other places
exist on the other side of them.

Open the door.
Break the glass.

Sleep on your roof tonight
so you can slumber to the heartbeat
of the stars.

You don't have to wait until tomorrow
to go to the edge of the earth.
You don't have to wait until
you are in your bed dreaming
before you wake up and
let go.

WHEN THE CLOCKS ATE TIME

It will start with the clocks.
They will eat time, slowly;
swallowing minutes,
gnawing off their hands.

Days will disintegrate next.
Followed by the words we call them.

The people will continue to go about their lives as we do.
We'll complain casually over coffee
about traffic and deadlines and the weather
and this and that and this and that...

We'll say that there never seems to be enough time
because the days keep disappearing
but we don't know where to?

The final step will be when
those bright slits in the night
begin to fall.

One by one
tired of watching us rush
through it all

This will be how the world will end.

We'll catch those delicate shining things
that rhyme with scars on our skin.
We'll notice everything then.
We'll wonder where it all went.
We'll wonder where we spent all that time.
But by then it will be too late
and we'll wonder how it all seemed to go by so quickly,
how it disappeared just like,
that...

Things that burn.
Wood.
Me.
Bridges.
The sun.

You.

Fingertips.
Cigarettes.
Skin.

WINTER

Words we've spoke.
Nights we've had.

This.
Tongues.
Beds.

The center of the earth.
Everything.

AMPHITRITE

Superimpose my reflection in your bones—
call me a masochist.

Wanna be so deep inside you
I can taste the tremble in your tendons,
marrow to membrane,
at 4:30am in the morning,
11:00pm on a Sunday.

Replicating a rapture with the friction in fingers.
I'll swallow your singsong then place a mockingbird in my mouth
in hopes that it will fly down my throat so I can croon you out.

Call me organist.
Evoke a symphony from our shivers,
strum the strings of our bodies like harps,
my spine will contain the chorus,
your pelvis the verse.

Move against me like the ocean,
girl with the mermaid hair.

Tentacles to tendrils.
We found each other in a shipwreck
confused by the attraction of our flesh and fins in the shrapnel.

We will whisper each other to dream with midnight manifestos.
I will tell you about Mississippi
if you tell me about growing up 1,743 miles underneath the sea.

Enthralled by our histories,
we will be the thing that people call myth.
They will want to dissect us so they can figure out how we fit.

Back to belly,
our bodies arched like the moon;
resenting the morning for splitting us in two.

You smell of firewood and sea foam.

Taste like a pear.
Taste like hazel.
Feel as delicate as fog.
Feel as warm as whiskey.

I want to kiss you as soft as a whisper.
I want to kiss your elbows and your nose
because I meant it when I told you

every part of you is beautiful.

Escape the city with me.
Like renegade stallions we'll outrun the engines,
rename the streets,
there is sapphire in our palms;
when we touch we burn peridot.

Let us roll ourselves tight
and sleep in the canvases
of Klimt and Magritte;
warm and full we will be.

Tentacle to tendril.
Marrow to membrane.

Practicing the proximity of bodies
for we both have found comfort in loneliness before

but not tonight.

Call me selfish
for wanting to set fire to the maps
so you won't return
to the sea.

COFFIN NAILS

Started smoking cigarettes because I got lonely.
They were the only things I could depend on.

There are lots of similarities between us and them;
we all can become addicting.

I realize this as I puff on a cigarette.

Sucking in quick as if oxygen doesn't come fast enough
and food is no longer a fuel that can fill me up
as much as you did doing nothing other than
being.

I am sorry.

I am sorry for whatever it was that happened,
for whatever it is I may be lacking,
but it is not my fault that I speak moon.

And it is not your fault that you read sun and stars
and sleep in a blanket created by ocean and fire,

but I will not let you use me as your floatation device
any longer than the time it takes me to smoke this cigarette.

I kicked the first habit, baby.
Put nicotine in your place.

But it is not because I don't love you,
or miss you.

It is because I'm lonely.

And these cigarettes are the only things I have left
to depend on.

ULTRASAURUS POEM
(THE ENCYCLOPEDIA SHOW OCT, 2011)

The paleontologists wanted your genus to be that of fact
so Dinosaur Jim went to dig up dirt,
looking for a spine to prove your existence.
Reconstruct your skyscraper neck to show
that 100 million years prior
you had reached the dirty ankles of God,
that you drank the rain before it ever left the sky.

You were 100 feet tall;
a swallower of stars,
wore a rainbow as your scarf.
Each step you took made the earth turn kickdrum,
made the earth thunderclap under your weighted walk.
You were one long trombone.
Your throat a slow anthem
that made the sun hum halo.

You were big, once.
A behemoth skeleton,
skin now a disintegrated mountain of ash,
evaporated dust left on the tailspin of a falling star,
shooting.

Your life was treetop and bark.
A humble hippy of the Jurassic period,
you were granola chomper;
vegan by default,
now left to rest in the graveyard of Dry Mesa Colorado with
bones being analyzed under the curiosity of human breath
and the science of microscopes.

We wanted you to be massive, so badly,
that we collected all the wrong bones
and called you,

Ultrasaurus! Mega lizard!!

The most elaborate nomen nudum for a chimera—
a mythical being we tried to bring to life
by fusing two opposing species together.

I don't blame them for trying.

It is only human
to want to make things fit.
We do this often.

It's the entwining of legs with people we know won't make sense
and when the dawn comes like a clean promise
we can still recognize the stain of evening
by the smell on our skin
we call human.

An animal burdened with so much clank
and rumble buried behind our breastplate
it takes a knife 18 tries to get to the heart of it.

We are the only species preoccupied with puzzles.
How we fantasize kings and romanticize the bottoms of oceans.
We've killed so many things in our explorations
but not you.

Oh Ultrasaurous!

You were here first.
Before bow and arrow
concrete, soda pop,
lighters, and men.

You were here before we began,
when God was a handsome lady who rode you bareback.

But now you and her are two resting ghosts
watching us try to make the dead fit.
Reconstruct your vertebrae back
while never noticing that what is alive dies a little everyday.

We will all be dinosaurs someday.

You are proof that even the grandest decay;
life only happens so long.
Death is just a moment when the living is done,
and when we are over,
I wonder if anyone would wish for our species to return.

FROM WHERE HE SLEEPS, THE SKY TASTES OF A CERTAIN COLOR THAT DOESN'T HAVE A NAME

Oh God,
look at what we've done to you and your sky.

Harness up the horses.
There is a storm the size of 10,000 fists rising from sand.
Lightning twists off the wind,
the sky is a talent show between countries
to see whose bombs pack more punch.
More Rocky,
Apollo,
Muhammad Ali.

Somewhere, the clouds are coughing up coffins
and shaking petals off flowers;
causing even the wild to howl up their prayers.

At night, he takes sleeping-pills the size of bullets
wishing for the day he can dream without one eye open.

Instincts should never smell like gunpowder.
This is not what it means to be human.

Every day he wakes to tie his shoestrings like nooses
so his feet won't shake as hard as his heart does.
The blood on his boots is as heavy as the tanks he's hid in
so he bulletproofs his soul and patrols the ground by foot.

Today marks the soldier's 422nd day
of waking up in this land of sand and sweat.
His lack of appetite has nothing to do
with the scent of scorched bodies
he watched coming from the mosque
his unit was ordered to arson
blown in by the western wind.

He doesn't eat because inhaling cigarettes
is easier than chewing food.
The children he sees scream

in the streets because they have no water
to wash the dried blood off their lips from where
they tried to kiss their mother and father's bodies back together.
Nas nothing to do with why his skin itches.
A bug bit him. He has become immune.
He cried for the first 24 days about what he had seen,
wanted to fast like Jesus for 40 but mortality got the best of him.

On day 17
he ate his own ribs, medium rare.
Pulled the meat from the bone with his teeth,
his conscience now falls out of his hand each time he salutes
or wipes his mouth clean.

Staring into the stars he wonders,
Why God would let his only begotten son be crucified for this
that if God created us in his image,
then God must really hate himself.

Every time he hears,
Soldier, straighten up!
He wants to release his finger from the trigger and run.

He is unable to pause the soundtrack of his commanders shouting,
The terrorists have no age. Shoot the children if you have to.
Let 'em see that their god is no match to our machines.

Thomas, the young boy turned toy soldier,
used to dress his 19-yr-old self up real nice
with dreams for his sleeves,
eyes facing northward,
because where he's from,
the Midwestern sky was the only thing clean.

The army was a promise for him to travel
to places no bigger than a finger on a map.
Now the same sky that used to lullaby him to sleep
is filled with filth of burned sinew and tissue,
so he hums himself to sleep
and pretends the bombs are wind-chimes.

He cannot hear the wish of his mother praying,
please come home,
because he is too busy shouting,
Sir, yes sir!

She wants him to return with the organs and limbs he left with.
She wants his tongue to still remember her name,
for his heart not to turn into sand paper.
Son!
Do not forget the shape of a hug.
Do not make your smile a martyr.

Since you have been sleeping with snipers
I fear your hands have become more familiar
with the pulling of triggers
than the song coming from the strum of heartstrings.

Tonight, Thomas isn't dreaming,
but writing in his coffin
a letter addressed to the moon
with a message to deliver to the heavens saying,

Why would you create us in your image Lord,
knowing we would be fighting for this?

THE PARTS OF HUMANS
THAT SCIENCE CAN'T EXPLAIN

There are parts of humans that science can't explain.

We know the mechanics of organs
and which way the blood flows.
We know the effects of smoking
and typical reactions to taste buds.

A scientist likes to think that in time he will know *everything*.

The problem with knowing everything
is that we often forget what is worth remembering.

The doctor sits me on a table
and asks me to stick out my tongue.
I do.

I ask him if he sees the paintings I carry
in the back of my throat.
He laughs as if I'm telling a joke,
I'm not.

I've got Basquiat, Schiele, Van Gogh, and Da Vinci
so when I laugh, I taste brushstrokes.

I ask him if he can stick out his tongue
so I can see what he has trapped inside of him.
He hesitates a little then he does
and I see a man who struggles for acceptance and chokes
on the word
love.

We've got robots that dismantle bombs
so soldiers can still pull triggers with their finger.
We've got a blueprint of a hotel
that will be located on the moon in 2047.

We've got microchips small enough
to be slipped inside of hair follicles
yet we still have a hard time
saying words like please and thank-you
and offering our hands to help strangers.

The psychiatrist asks me what I am feeling
so she can prescribe me a pill

to take that feeling away,
as if that will solve something.

I sit there silent, hoping not to interfere with
the tambourines and trumpets being played in my head.

She stares in my eyes and I hope
that she can see my insides dancing
but I can tell by the sigh in her face
that she hasn't danced in a long, long time.

This is what we are creating.

A world where the living and breathing
are dependant on inanimate objects that only move
because they have buttons and batteries
when we have hearts.

I go to school to make sense of this,
to find the formula that will save us,
when my professor instructs me to lift
my head from my desk and quit sleeping.

I tell him,

I'm not sleeping, I'm dreaming—
There's a difference.

I ask him if he dreams and he tells me
that there isn't enough time for that
when we have work to do.

So I take out my pen and paper and I draw him what I dream;
it is people who sleep in rainclouds,
pass out more smiles than business cards,
and find beauty in the broken things.

It is people who can speak every language
so we can better understand each other.
While he continues his lecture about
the greatest inventions of the 21st century.

All the students in the class speak excitedly about
iPhones, satellite radios, and plasma screen TVs
that can help us see things more clearly.

This world that we are living in seems more foreign to me
than Pluto's moons or the idea of being a queen.

With every great advancement we make it seems like
we are taking something more important back.

Like we are trying to prove to ourselves that we are smarter
than monkeys and apes because we can build skyscrapers and send
rockets to space.

To each his own seems to be our motto
and since this is the case

I wish the aliens would come attack us today.

Because only then would we unite as one world,
instead of being separated by our own
governments, prejudices, religions, and races.

And only then would we may be able to figure out
The parts of humans that science can't explain.

FOR BILLY

A throat is a harp full of strings
meant to be strummed,
not cut.
The body, a song spilling of sea and hum.

Billy,
when I read how they found you
dangling in the barn,
I wanted to know who told you your neck
was a branch to swing from.

I know what it's like to think your skin
is made of shingles, but you were
no roof to jump from,
kid.

This is for anyone being told to live in a shadow.
Crack the glow-sticks in your halo,
burn so beautiful that if the sun
ever looked at you he'd go blind.
There is no bully out there bright enough
to dim your shine.

Billy,
just because you loved a boy
didn't mean your town should have
tried to straighten your notes
when your throat has always been a harp to strum and
never a branch to be found swinging from.

GRAVITY OF STARS

Discovered while staring at the bottom of a coffee-cup
that I've spent too much time looking-up.
That if your head is arched too high in the clouds
you can't appreciate how much you have grown
once you have forgotten the ground.

I want to forget about stars.
About things that fly.
Skyscrapers.
Superheroes.
And God.

I want to find magnitude in a molehill,
hard work on an ant's back,
bad choice in an empty bottle,
forgiveness in a person's car wreck.
I want to see color the same way a blind man must feel it.

Tell me when it was I forgot about simplicity.
When I started to believe that someone
who could do trigonometry in their head mattered more
than a 33-year-old man who finally woke up this morning
and decided he was done wasting his life.
Today, he was gonna figure out how to be better at living.

We need to remember to go up
to every person we see with scars,
shake their hand and say,
Congratulations for surviving whatever it was
that caused you to hurt yourself.

Stop wishing on stars and start believing in ourselves again.

This world is a ticking time bomb;
everyday that passes is just another moment less.

I want to see my reflection in an eye of a fly.
No more stargazing.
Waterfall wishing.
Prayer giving.

I'm starting to get a crook in my neck
by staring in the clouds for too long.
I want to be inspired by heartbeats again.
Hold people like my favorite book,

kiss the fat pimple on a teenager's forehead and say,
I hope you don't think that is a factor in how beautiful you are,
'Cuz it is not.

Tell Michael Ray Stevens,
It doesn't make you bad to be in love with a boy—
love is what makes us human.
Be happy that you feel something for someone—
you'd be surprised how difficult that is for some.

I want to tell pilots to try swimming.
That the sky is way too beautiful for us to be in it.
We need to come down from our high-horse.

Tomorrow I'm going to travel Austin, TX by crawling on my knees
in hopes that when I stand back up I'll see things differently.

I'm done dreaming of astronauts.
The moon is a made-up romantic.

Put me in the pavement.
Lie my carcass in the cracks.
Let me be humbled by the power
of speaking by the silent dance
of a deaf man's hands.

I want to watch closely the lips of a mute
who wishes for nothing other than to hear
the sound of his voice.

Visit a hospital and hold the hand
of a woman in a coma dreaming
about moving again.

For the sky has nothing in it as interesting
as the diversity on this earth.
That is why I don't care anymore about flying.

There is a reason the stars keep falling.
They are jealous of the things we get to see
by being here—
on
the
ground...

Wanted to rest
in your tendrils.
Be an upside down pistol,
loaded and cocked

SPRING

with something
more beautiful than the
sum of your atoms multiplied
by the whole of my parts.

THE GARDENER

In your bones I'll grow flowers
so you can pick the
love me,
love me nots
out of your chest
in hopes that in the last petal
you will find yourself.

Tell me stories.

Tell me of the times you went searching for
mystics and pots of gold at the end of rainbows,
asked for a waterbed for Christmas because
you thought that it would make you feel more like
the Little Mermaid and less like
everyone else.

When was the day that you looked at yourself and cried
because you didn't understand your face anymore;
those freckles are just signs that the sun
finds you irresistible,
and every wrinkle you get represents
something far more beautiful and truthful
than any poem I'll ever have the ability or courage to write.

Give me your vampires,
your nightmares,
every bit of baggage on your back.
Give me your monsters,
bad tastes, and bit lips.

Stand still.

Let me figure out the math from which your bones grow
with the soft part of my hands,
finding colors in your organs,
pulling music from your ribs.
trying to understand
why you go searching for things
that never left you to begin with?

Why you wait for messengers
to fall from the sky and pick up your prayers
as if you couldn't answer them yourself?
There are things far more important inside of you

than the greatest hymns and equations.
Don't think that just because
you don't have the answers now
means you never will.

Because not all questions have remedies,
not all stars have names,
and not every lover feels the same.

But we all feel.

And what affects you might not affect me,
and I might not be able to understand
where you're coming from sometimes,
but I can be there to hear you
when you feel like the entire world
has forgotten your name.

I can be there like a surprise at the end of the day,
when you feel change doesn't exist
and everything and everyone is the same.

I will come.

Bearing shovels in my whispers,
planting flowers in your bones,
so when you laugh there may be petals in your giggles;
reminding you of the beautiful things you may have forgotten
that are growing inside you still.

MOUNTAINS ON THE MOON

We were ambitious stargazers
the night you told me that there were mountains on the moon.

In that ember evening
you taught me how to dance just by smiling
so I replaced walking with waltzing
and made it a point to taste the rain.

I took a nose dive into risky,
knew it was danger the first time I saw you.
My conscience told me you were going to
burn me like a roman candle,
fry me like an egg,
sunny-side all fucked up.
I put my fists down, burnt my guardrail and said,
Come on! I want you to sucker-punch me toothless—
I'm not afraid of this.

Wanted to be beaten brutally beautiful,
follow your sidewinder,
get lost in the thunder of your storm.
You told me that I shouldn't be attracted
to disasters,
but I responded,
If that's the case then mistakes are for learning—
I want you to teach me something.

You kissed me until my lips bled Valentine's Day.
I shot up like redemption,
we made love all night;
I drew your favorite constellation with my tongue
on the part of your body you hated.

You asked,
Do you know what happens when you squeeze sand?

Wanted to say that you should stop thinking in hourglasses.
Set fire to your reservations and run with me forward
instead of living in your past.

But you pushed my hands away and explained,
You should have never touched me
as if I had a heartbeat.
I'm not used to it.

She is the red in the rainbow.
My heart was a trench I let her fall into
but the thing about ghosts
is that they cannot be buried;
she escaped my dirt.

I understand now what she meant by mountains on the moon,
but if she were to come back I would remind her that
the craters is the reason it burns beautiful.

THE MARBLE FARM

You may think that this is a fairytale, but it isn't.
This is a true story, and it goes like this:

The marble farm came the year
the stars had turned their insides woolen
during the snowglow burn of evening.

Moonmist fell into a hole,
hence bloomed the marble people.

They had marble eyes and marble hands.
Marble laughs and marble legs.

On the other side of the mountain lived the brick people,
who thought them odd, thought them strange
so they kept them at a distance,
fearful of their difference.

Even though the marble people
worked hard both night and day
they still found time to laugh and love and play.

The brick people made fun of them and deemed them poor,
but the marble folk didn't understand
since they had a thing called happy inside of 'em.

The brick people were strange too
with their brick heads and brick homes,
brick hearts and brick bones.
But the marble people
didn't believe that just because someone was different
meant that you should be mean and treat them poorly.

Why am I telling you all of this? You may ask.
Well so you can better understand what happened next.

Marlee was a girl who grew up at the marble farm,
but there was something unique about her.
She was born with this peculiar thing
that no one seemed to have
called wonder.

One day she woke up and decided
she wanted to see for herself
what life was like on the other side of the mountain.

Her family was sad and scared but they understood
that sometimes one has to see for themselves
what it's like to be somewhere else.

Marlee ate a piece of marble bread
before she packed everything up in her marble bag.

When she got to the brick road a brick person told her
that she needed to go back home,

but Marlee stared confused
by how the man didn't know that we all contain
a piece of home no matter where we go.

Marlee soon found out that the
brick people build and they build and they build
because they believe that having lots of things
makes them wealthy.

Perhaps this may be true
but she noticed that no one in the brick town
took time to laugh or play,
and if you never do those things than you have a
hard time finding love, or ever being happy.

A little brick boy came up to her and asked,
Why are you made so weird?

Marlee laughed and said,
I suppose I could ask you the same thing.

The boy grinned,
You aren't that scary, He said.

Why would I be? She asked.

*I don't know. That's what my family tells me. They say your kind
are poor and lazy. That ya'll don't build anything. Ya'll just stare
at the stars and dream.*

*Well that's not entirely true, boy. But even if it were,
what would be so wrong with that?
You are partially right, though, we do not build things
because being made of marble we'd rather polish what we have.*

The boy didn't know what to say so he just shook his head

Come with me boy! Marlee said.

And do what?

Anything you want!
We can jump on the stars and climb the night. Or we can go to the place
where wishes float. I can show you what it's like to laugh and play.

No, no I can't! He screamed and then ran away.

Marlee went back to the Marble Farm sad and confused
for she didn't understand why the brick people
spent so much time working and being afraid.

Marlee is an old, old woman now,
but still thinks about that day.

She wonders about that boy
and how many others are still out there
who don't know how much fun life can be
when you take the time to
laugh and love and play.

A CONDITION CALLED FEELING

You know, they say I was born with this condition.
The doctor told my mom, *I'm afraid your baby was born with too much 'feeling'.*

She said she cried even though she didn't know exactly what he meant except that having a child with too many feelings sounded hard to protect.

When I was nine I tried to peel the white from my flesh because I didn't like the history from which it came.

Once, I actually felt the fist someone threw through the face of a boy they called faggot some 700 miles away.

My mom brought me a bag of ice, put it over my eye, and told me that the world wasn't mine to save.

I was never impressed with superheros, just regular people who did incredible things.

I was a weird kid who thumbtacked pictures of Einstein, Martin Luther King, Marilyn Monroe, and Beethoven to my wall.

I thought that the magnitude behind their impact could be attributed to how much they felt.

How else would you explain the way Beethoven played even though he couldn't hear a thing.

Or how Martin Luther King always spoke for what he believed in spite of all the hatred that he and his family received.

How they all must have stared at both their faces and the stars wondering how each day contains so much beauty, yet so much pain. But how necessary it is to feel it all anyway.

I often wonder how many people have taken the time to stare in awe at the sunset? Do you remember how it felt the first time you saw it?

Have you ever shed a tear by seeing something so gorgeous that it suddenly made life incredibly all worth it?

How about the way your lover's lips hit you like a home-run, or the hurt that happened when she moved on even though you didn't.

We're all gonna have our sick days and heartbreaks.

The trick is stitching stars on the inside of your eyelids to help you see the brightside of things.

Even when you break, know that it doesn't make you broken as much as it creates you into one beautiful jigsaw of human.

I believe that when we are born, we don't come out speaking, but feeling for a reason. Crying instantly at how terrifying yet beautiful this thing called life can be.

Feeling isn't something we should fear, or view as an attribute to the weak. For it is a wondrous gift and I think that life without it would be a horrible thing.

LIBRARY LUNATICS

Visit a library with me!

Let's lose ourselves in the fiction section,
play lost and found in the R thru Z aisle.
I wanna guess what book you pick up
based off the line you read me.
We can use our imaginations
and pretend to be someone else for awhile.

Re-enact a play on the 3rd floor,
role-play fairytales on the 7th,
close our eyes and pretend we are flying.
We can be gypsies, pirates, kings, and queens.
We can be Virginia Woolf, James Tate, Lorca, Plath, and Capote.

Forget our fingers in the pages.

Your eyes look like they are breathing
once you've lost yourself
in the words you're reading.
There are flames in these stories
like there is aliveness in our breath.

There is a delicate amber glow in the section we are in, the light bulbs
are happy to be here, they are happy to show us the books. And I'm feeling
inspired and defeated by being surrounded in this swamp of genius.

I want to kiss you on the pleat in between your eyebrows and ask you to
make me a suggestion as to what hardback I should add to my collection.
I want you to read me the first page of the story in my bed, underneath
the covers, with just the lamp on, put my ear to your chest and rest
while my heartbeat mimics your meter.

Linguistic lovers. Erudite etymologists. Page pedantics.
We are aficionados of the alphabet!

Hold my hand and follow me to the bathroom
because we are going to scribble on the stalls,
scrawl our favorite words down, definitions and all.
Let's highlight the halls,
tattoo the toilets with passages from poets,
graffiti the ground, stain it with statements,
and make our mark by declaring to the world
what we think of it.

You and I are word-warriors and literary lunatics.
Instead of book-burnings we are going to start television fires.

This library is our chapel.

There is so much knowledge to absorb, but neither of us will ever be
able to do it because no one can, and that's okay. We will still keep our
minds open.

I tell you that we should bring our sleeping-bags next time, crawl atop
the rafters, and sleep above the languages so we can dream another
country.

Your eyes get big and hesitant because you know I'm serious as you put
your finger over my mouth and say *psssh we are in a library! And I yell
yes, I know! I was the one who brought you here. It's called a library date!*

You playfully nudge me and I run off
to find another story to get drunk off of.
I find myself absorbed in Frederico Garcia Lorca,
sipping on his stanzas, getting inebriated off his intellect.

I look up and see you critiquing a classic.
You always do that.
You find the flaws in things.

I think about how sad I'll be the day you will leave me.
So I go back to my book trying to escape the thought of you leaving,
wanting to lose myself in these pages,
and wishing that all along
I was the one you wanted to get lost with.

SKELETON KEY

Got a lockbox in my chest.
It fits underneath my ribcage,
a little left of my heart.

It pivots and shakes. *Pivots and shakes.*

Tends to keep the things it shouldn't,
throwing the parts it needs away.
All I've got are fragments of faces.
Goosebumps of past lover's hands.

Tell the girl who thinks she may be in love with me
to forget my name before the moon makes room for the morning.

We will be hands missing palms.
Singed eyelids.
Nonsensical time-zones.
Submerged matches.
An untitled painting hung in a hallway.

This is what we will be.
Half-awake. Fully-alive,
fumbling for our zippers wanting to make sense of it all.
Touching each other until our shadows shout,
smiling because we can't understand
what we don't want to figure out.

We will be disintegrated erasers
because we couldn't get it right the first time.

Come morning,
I will be your final bad habit.

Come morning,
we will call each other distance.

I will still remember your scent
even after you have forgotten mine.

FREE FALL

The first time I saw her
I had lost all the words.

I had somehow fallen tongue over toes.
My heartbeat broke out in a sad stutter.
My jaw was full of bees.

When she walked up to me I was as awkward
as a first kiss. All I knew to say was, *Hello.*
It was as if I was speaking for the first time
and she was a language I did not know.

On our first date
I told her I was gonna build us a starsling,
stitch the stars myself.

She asked if that's how we'd get to the moon.
I said, *No, but it'll help us travel through space.*
She laughed and said I was full of shit.
And I proudly informed here,
Well, we all are., this is why we poop.

This was the beginning of us.
The skeptic and the mystic,
two mismatched lovers caught up in our own spells.

I used to think nothing mattered but magic in a romance.
What I've learned
is that it takes much more
to make a relationship work.
We are one troubling equation
that no one has figured out
even though we've gone through many steps,
and I feel like we're on the right path,
we just stumble on the math sometimes.

I've never been good with numbers.
I always forgot what the signs meant.
But you don't have to know very much to feel how
it hurts to be subtracted.
I never wanted to call her ghost.
I didn't want her to become another haunting.

Maybe I should have been more cautious
and rubbed sunscreen on my heart

before she could burn it.

I don't know why I always seem to fall for arsonists.

Perhaps my first mistake was saying thank you to
the first compliment she ever gave me
instead of taking the forewarning
that what people are most attracted to
is an attribute they don't possess.

I never believed for a second that we would last long...

Just longer.

It takes an awful amount of time to make love to someone
who doesn't like themselves.

I can speak from experience when I say
you can spend your whole life running but in the end
the only thing that gets you is tired.

Bravery isn't fleeing.
It's kissing the teeth of something
you know could eat you in an instant.

How stupid it is to run away from something that might
be the greatest thing that you've ever encountered
just because you are too afraid that it might not work out.

Taking chances is how we grow.
It's how we understand ourselves.

And love might be the riskiest chance of all
but it is not a game;
it's a test.

It's a bridge you leap from
without worry if the cord will hold you back or snap.
In spite of the outcome it will be
one helluva free-fall.

SHADOWBOXER

There is a suitcase I keep in my sternum.
One night when I was loading my heartcontents,
packing myself up as I've done more times than I'd care to admit,
I stopped myself mid-zipper at the breastplate and asked,

*How many more places do you have to go before you realize
that the only thing running gets you is tired?*

18 countries,
4 cartons of smokes,
and a trashcan full of
filthy hangovers and painful goodbyes later—
I realize that you can leave from many places,
but you cannot leave yourself.

I've woken up many mornings bruised and broken
from fist-fighting with my own shadow
over things I can't control
and stuff I don't want to.

I don't believe we hate ourselves;
it's just that it's hard to determine
the parameters of how much we love.

Before Ophelia took a nose dive to see
what was swimming at the bottom
of that wishing well
she said,

We know who we are, but not who we may be.

There are things we know by feeling,
and there are things we know by thought.

I know a blue whale has a heart the size of a Volkswagen van.
A heart so big one could build a home in
yet we still kill it for its skin.

I know that even though Egyptians slept on pillows made of stone
they still dreamt of pyramids and built them when they woke up.

I know Basquiet slept in gutters just to feel closer to the rain
and that water isn't always needed for things to grow,
somethings thrive in shade.

I know that if the only direction you have to go is everywhere,
the chances of you getting lost are slim.

That bad things can happen no matter where you are—
so can good.

And we should all learn to be a little better at being more aware.

We can't hold it all no matter how hard we try.
That the strongest muscles aren't used for staying
but for saying goodbye.
It's taking the broken and rebuilding it into something
that even a wrecking ball can't crumble.

Tell me how it came to be that perfection
is a lie too many people have died believing in?

When the most beautiful things I've seen
have always been the flawed.

It's the stuff that doesn't make sense
that can be the most intriguing.

Aword can hit you so hard
that even your arm hairs start to stutter,
or the last I love you you hear in the dying breath of your mother.

I think it's natural for us to be a little afraid of some things,
but the trick is to not let whatever fear you may have hold you back
from becoming what it is that you can be.

We should all strive to be box-breakers,
never afraid to rise;
even if what is holding you back
is something inside of yourself—
don't let your own shadow be the thing that
strangles how bright you can shine.

THE CHANGING OF SEASONS

Have you ever wondered how sometimes
a person can make you feel heavy?

Not heavy like you just scarfed down 2 Brooklyn style pizzas
chased down with a 6 pack of Lonestar.

I'm talking about heavy like you just swallowed a season.

Heavy like you just took a big bite out of the sky
hoping to swallow that flock of bluebirds
so they can build a nest in the heartbreak
where your last love took off.

I did a detox cleanse once to try to get the weight out.
I had so much spit and sweat of yours still left in me
that it sunk my pores.

The *mourning* of day 4

I counted the 17 I love you's you said to me
in the toilet. It looked like alphabet soup;
A rotten diet. I lived on you like a beautiful
language I didn't understand a word of

Je t'aime
Te amo
Te iubesc
Ich liebe dich
أحبك

Jordan.

You share the same name of a war-torn country
and I can't help but wonder if that explains
all the battling between us.

Maybe we just can't help it.
Maybe the make-up sex is just that good.
I wanna take refuge in you like a bomb-shelter
that is if we don't blow each other up first
with all this bickering.

There are only so many
I am sorry. I didn't mean to hurt you,
that a person can take.

I have a good heart.
It doesn't understand why we couldn't
get this to work.

I didn't eat for weeks after we split
not because I wasn't hungry,
it was just that I was so full on emptiness
that I didn't have room for anything else.

Until the day I said enough with this fasting,
and put autumn in my mouth.
I felt the bluebirds fly south.
It was the season you left.

They built a nest in my chest where
your head used to be.

I'm glad that it happened, but
Im looking forward to the spring.
When all this deadweight is lifted,
when I'm able to finally get over you,
and not think so much about how perfect
we used to be.

ACKNOWLEDGEMENTS

I'd like to give a heartfelt thank you to the Austin Poetry Slam. If you didn't exist, neither would I. Thank you to all of my fellow poets and pals who come to APS on a regular basis, and also to the fresh faced folks who come to listen and/or perform. You all are the beat in the heart that keeps this little thing called poetry pumping. ;)

Bill Moran thanks for writing in a way that makes language dance and for helping me with all those wonderful music accompaniments. I couldn't have done it without you. You are truly a good ghost who brings the good news.

Danny Strack you deserve much more credit than you allow yourself to take. Thank you for caring about community and poetry because that is what it should always be about.

Zachary Caballero quit writing poetry that makes all the girls swoon for you. It makes me jealous. ;)

Tova Charles, chip- chip- cheerio!! I'm so glad I know you.

Kevin Burke I like your appreciation of Jameson and that you write good shit. Both of those things make me very, very happy.

Ebony Stewart thank you for all of your love and support.

Steph Smith thank you are my bff for this life and the next and even the one after that. I'd do anything for you. You are the best!

Featherbottom Bushytail thank you moving into the No-Tell Motel. Living there wouldn't have been half as fun without you.

Lauren Bradshaw you are an asshole which is my affectionate way of saying that I count you as a good friend. You knew me in the days before dreadlocks.

Sterling Wilkerson thank you for knowing so much more about things I do not.

Alex Russell thank you for not being afraid of moving into a house with a broken legged person and accepting my addiction to breakfast tacos. I couldn't ask for a better roommate.

To the rest of my friends, you already know who you are, thank you for putting up with me on a regular basis.

Timber Mouse thank you for publishing this collection of poems I never thought would leave my bedroom.

Thank you to any and everyone who is reading this now. It puts one beaming grin on my face to know that my words are in your hands in this very moment. It's like you are hugging me all over. I can feel it.

And finally, I'd like to give a roaring thank you to Austin for being a city full of beautiful ladies. Seriously. My deepest gratitude goes to you all. I wouldn't have half as many poems if I didn't fall in love nearly every time I left my house.

ABOUT THE AUTHOR

Lacey Roop is a
nationally recognizd
and touring poet placing
6th in the 2011 Women
of the World Poetry
Slam (WOWPS), was the
Austin, TX Individual
World Poetry Slam
(IWPS) representative,
and has been a two-
time member of the
renowned Austin Poetry
Slam.

What is far more in-
teresting about Lacey,
however, is that she has
an uncanny ability to get hit by cars while biking, finds the fact
that we are all made of stars both fascinating and comforting, and wears a
key around her neck that unlocks the bottom of the ocean.
Really, it does :)

www.laceyroop.com